THE WASHINGTON REDSKINS

Sloan MacRae

PowerKiDS press™

New York

Published in 2011 by The Rosen Publishing Group, Inc.
29 East 21st Street, New York, NY 10010

Copyright © 2011 by The Rosen Publishing Group, Inc.

First Edition

Editor: Amelie von Zumbusch
Book Design: Greg Tucker
Layout Design: Julio Gil

Photo Credits: Cover (DeAngelo Hall), p. 21 Larry French/Getty Images; cover (Charley Taylor), p. 15 Focus on Sport/Getty Images; cover (Sammy Baugh), pp. 11, 22 (top) Bruce Bennett Studios/Getty Images; cover (background) Doug Pensinger/Getty Images; p. 5 Scott Cunningham/Getty Images; p. 7 Kevin C. Cox/Getty Images; p. 9 Scott Boehm/Getty Images; p. 13 Nate Fine/NFL/Getty Images; p. 17, 22 (bottom) Ronald C. Modra/Sports Imagery/Getty Images; p. 19 Andy Hayt/Getty Images.

Library of Congress Cataloging-in-Publication Data

MacRae, Sloan.
   The Washington Redskins / by Sloan MacRae. — 1st ed.
      p. cm. — (America's greatest teams)
   Includes index.
   ISBN 978-1-4488-3169-2 (library binding) — ISBN 978-1-4488-3176-0 (pbk.) —
   ISBN 978-1-4488-3177-7 (6-pack)
   1. Washington Redskins (Football team)—History—Juvenile literature. I. Title.
   GV956.W3M34 2011
   796.332'6409753—dc22
                              2010039431

Manufactured in the United States of America

CPSIA Compliance Information: Batch #WW11PK: For Further Information contact Rosen Publishing, New York, New York at 1-800-237-9932

CONTENTS

UPS AND DOWNS

The Washington Redskins are one of the most important teams in all of American sports because they play in the Washington, D.C., area. Washington, D.C., is the nation's **capital**. It is also one of America's biggest cities. This means that the Redskins have lots of fans.

The Redskins are one of the oldest teams in the National Football **League**, or the NFL. They have lots of history. Most of their history is good. They have also played through many hard years at the bottom of the NFL, though. Happily, great players and **coaches** helped the Redskins climb back to the top.

Redskins fans show their love for the team in many ways. Some dress up as hogs. This is because a group of great Redskins players from the 1980s was called the Hogs.

WHAT'S IN A NAME?

The Redskins get their name from an old word for Native Americans, or American Indians. People used to say that Native Americans had red skin. Not everyone likes the Redskins' name. Many people believe it makes fun of Native American **culture**. Others believe that the name honors Native Americans. They say that the name was picked because Native Americans were known for being strong. The football team is strong.

The Redskins' colors are gold, white, and a special shade of red called burgundy. Every NFL team has its own **logo**. The Redskins' logo is a drawing of a Native American.

The Redskins' helmets have their logo on the sides. As you can see, the picture of the Native American is in a circle with two feathers on one side.

HAIL TO THE REDSKINS

The Redskins play in a **stadium** called FedEx Field. It gets its name from the shipping company FedEx. The Redskins have lots of fans. It is a good thing that FedEx Field has thousands of seats! In fact, FedEx Field holds several NFL records for the most football fans at games. These fans often dress up like Native Americans. Some even paint their faces.

The Redskins are one of the only teams in the NFL to have a **marching band**. The band often plays a song called "**Hail** to the Redskins." Fans sing along with the band. This makes FedEx Field a very loud place to be during games!

Here, members of the Redskins Marching Band are playing before a Redskins game. The marching band was formed in 1937.

THE BRAVES

The Washington Redskins were not always the Washington Redskins. The team was formed in 1932, in Boston, Massachusetts. It shared a stadium with a baseball team called the Braves. The teams shared more than a stadium. They were also both called the Braves!

The football Braves moved to Boston's Fenway Park in 1933. This is the home of a baseball team called the Boston Red Sox. The Braves changed their name to the Redskins.

The Redskins moved to Washington, D.C., in 1937. **Quarterback** Sammy Baugh led them to their first NFL **championship** in the same year. They won a second championship in 1942.

Sammy Baugh (center) was known as Slingin' Sammy because he was so good at throwing the ball. Passing became a more important part of football thanks to him.

11

A LONG DRY SPELL

The Redskins stayed on top of the NFL until the mid-1940s. In 1945, they lost a very close championship game to the Cleveland Rams. It took the Redskins a long time to come back after that. They entered one of the longest dry spells in American sports history. A team goes through a dry spell when it fails to win a championship for many years. Washington would not reach the **play-offs** again until the 1970s.

Even during their dry spell, the Redskins had some great players. They needed strong leaders, though. Washington fans would have to wait a long time before their team returned to greatness.

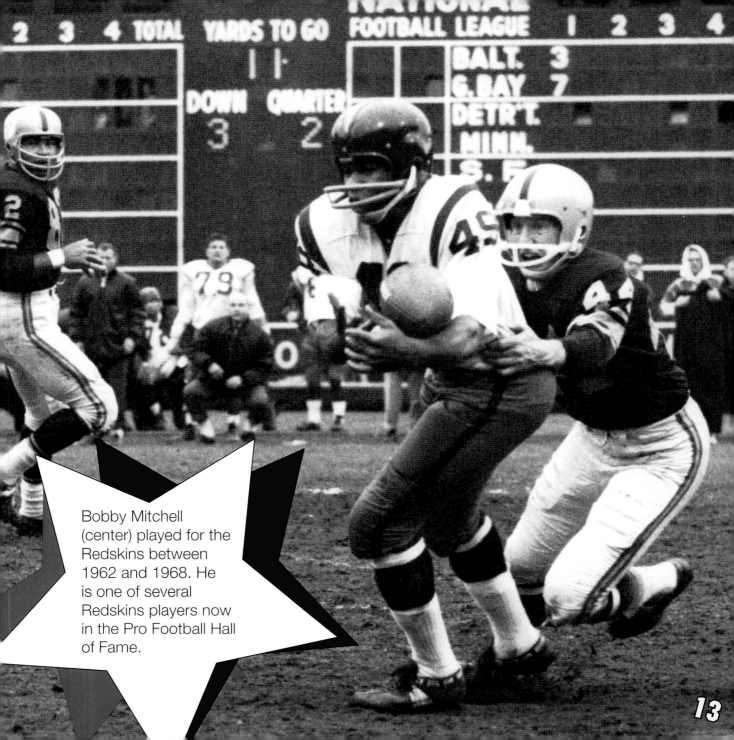

Bobby Mitchell (center) played for the Redskins between 1962 and 1968. He is one of several Redskins players now in the Pro Football Hall of Fame.

13

GEORGE ALLEN

The Redskins found the leader they needed in head coach George Allen. He joined the team in 1971. Luckily, he had talented players, such as Charley Taylor and Sonny Jurgensen, to work with. Allen turned the Redskins into winners in just one year. They reached the play-offs for the first time since 1945.

The Redskins were even better in Allen's second season. Allen led Washington to its first **Super Bowl**. The Redskins lost to an excellent Miami Dolphins team. Still, George Allen had done his job. It took a long time, but the Redskins were once again a great team.

Charley Taylor played wide receiver for the Redskins. Here he is running with the ball during the Super Bowl in 1973, in which the Redskins lost to the Dolphins.

JOE GIBBS

Allen's Redskins were good, but they had yet to win a Super Bowl. The Redskins hoped to change this when they hired Joe Gibbs as their head coach in 1981. Gibbs would soon become one of the greatest coaches in NFL history. **Running back** John Riggins also became a team leader. He helped the Redskins reach the Super Bowl in 1983. They faced the Dolphins once again. This time, though, the Redskins won!

Washington returned to the Super Bowl in 1988. This time around, they beat the Denver Broncos. Doug Williams became the first African-American starting quarterback to win a Super Bowl.

Riggins (wearing number 44) and quarterback Joe Theismann (in number 7) were two of the Redskins' top players in the 1970s and 1980s.

17

CHANGES

Gibbs and the Redskins won a third Super Bowl in 1992. This time, they beat the Buffalo Bills. Gibbs left the team in 1993. Many fans believe that Gibbs is the best coach in NFL history.

The Redskins struggled without Gibbs. They entered another dry spell. They fielded a team with many of the greatest players in the NFL. Once again, though, they needed a strong leader. They made the play-offs again at the end of the 1999 season. However, they lost to the Tampa Bay Buccaneers in the second round. Gibbs returned to coach the team in 2004. He helped the Redskins return to the play-offs at the ends of the 2005 and 2007 seasons.

Quarterback Mark Rypien's great playing helped the Redskins win the Super Bowl in 1992. He was named the game's most valuable player, or MVP.

NEW LEADERS

The Redskins prove that a team is only as good as its leaders. Some of the NFL's best players have been Redskins. However, the team has won championships only behind strong coaches.

The Redskins got a great new coach in 2010 when Mike Shanahan joined the team. Former Philadelphia Eagles star Donovan McNabb became the Redskins' starting quarterback in the same year. Washington also has great team leaders in **defensive** star DeAngelo Hall and running back Clinton Portis. The Redskins have the leaders they need to win more championships. The fans at FedEx Field trust that the team's dry spells are behind it.

DeAngelo Hall joined the Redskins in 2008. He quickly became a key member of the team's defense.

WASHINGTON REDSKINS TIMELINE

1932

The Boston Braves football team is formed.

1937

The Redskins win their first championship by beating the Chicago Bears.

1945

The Redskins lose the championship game to the Cleveland Rams. They enter a long dry spell.

1952

Quarterback Sammy Baugh plays his last game.

1955

The Redskins make history by scoring 21 points against the Philadelphia Eagles in just over 2 minutes.

1971

George Allen leads the Redskins to their first play-off game since 1945.

1983

Gibbs and the Redskins beat the Miami Dolphins and win Washington's first Super Bowl.

1992

The Redskins win their third Super Bowl by beating the Buffalo Bills.

2010

Mike Shanahan becomes the head coach of the Redskins.

GLOSSARY

CAPITAL (KA-pih-tul) The city where a state's or country's government is based.

CHAMPIONSHIP (CHAM-pee-un-ship) Official naming of the best or winner.

COACHES (KOHCH-ez) People who direct teams.

CULTURE (KUL-chur) The beliefs, practices, and arts of a group of people.

DEFENSIVE (DEE-fent-siv) Playing in a position that tries to keep the other team from scoring.

HAIL (HAYL) A greeting with honor.

LEAGUE (LEEG) A group of sports teams.

LOGO (LOH-goh) A picture, words, or letters that stand for a team or company.

MARCHING BAND (MAHRCH-ing BAND) A band that plays music and marches at the same time.

PLAY-OFFS (PLAY-ofs) Games played after the regular season ends to see who will play in the championship game.

QUARTERBACK (KWAHR-ter-bak) A football player who directs the team's plays.

RUNNING BACK (RUN-ing BAK) A football player whose job is to take or catch the ball and run with it.

STADIUM (STAY-dee-um) A place where sports are played.

SUPER BOWL (SOO-per BOHL) The championship game of NFL football.

INDEX

WEB SITES

Due to the changing nature of Internet links, PowerKids Press has developed an online list of Web sites related to the subject of this book. This site is updated regularly. Please use this link to access the list:
www.powerkidslinks.com/teams/fredskins/